THE WONDER OF MIDDLE SCHOOL

JOHN MICHAEL LA FAUCI II

The Wonder of Middle School
Copyright © 2023 John Michael LaFauci II

Visit our website at
www.StillwaterPress.com
for more information.

First Stillwater River Publications Edition

ISBN: 978-1-960505-65-1

1 2 3 4 5 6 7 8 9 10

Written by John Michael LaFauci II.
Edited by Joan LaFauci.
Published by Stillwater River Publications,
West Warwick, RI, USA.

The WONDER of MIDDLE SCHOOL

Acknowledgements

A special thanks to my wife Joan, who helped with all the editing of this book and everything else I have written. Her help with all my work has made the writing process so much easier. This new endeavor for me started after I retired from education. It took quite a long time before I felt comfortable putting my thoughts on paper. Hopefully, the readers will find this short book an easy, fun read and realize the trials of most middle school students today and into the future. Education in our schools is changing at such a rapid rate that some of the topics in this book could very well be irrelevant not long after one reads this. We need to constantly be willing to adapt and improve the things we do when educating our young children. At times, it seems as though we are fighting a losing battle. Let's all keep our chins up and fight the good fight to ensure that our children get the best possible education possible, now and going forth.

Introduction

Before you start reading this book, it might be pru-dent for me to let you know what my qualifications are to write a book on the craziness of middle school. I was a middle school/high school history teacher in the Warwick School System for twenty years, followed by eight years as a Middle School Assistant Principal in Cumberland and North Providence, Rhode Island. My wife of fifty-two years was a junior high school English teacher for twenty-three years and a high school guidance counselor for her last five years in the city of Cranston, Rhode Island. My mom was a first-grade teacher in Cranston for thirty-eight years. My son taught at a special school for behaviorally challenged boys, and my daughter is a high school psychologist in the Smithfield School System.

Having thus been directly or indirectly a part of the education system in this country for a long time, I feel confident that I can write an honest, forthright assessment of what middle school is really like. You may disagree with some parts, and that is your right as the reader. Some parts may seem embellished, but I assure you, they are occurrences that happened.

I have decided that the best way to present this subject is by dividing the book into short chapters. Each chapter will be a topic all its own. There are so many different life experiences that affect the development of middle school students that it would be confusing to write it all down in a flowing synopsis.

There are some serious topics and many more humorous ones. I hope that both will allow you to understand how those three years affect an adolescent's life.

Before I delve into the many interesting subjects surrounding middle school students and their progression from elementary school to high school, it would be prudent to explain the history of the changes that have occurred in K-12 education over the past fifty years.

During the 1950s and early 60s, many households were one-income families with Dad at work while Mom stayed home, tending to the house and children. For this reason, many of the elementary schools were neighborhood-based. The child would walk to school in the morning. Those students in the lower grades would be escorted by their moms until it became too embarrassing for the child to be seen holding their mom's hand in public. Because Mom was, for the most part, still at home, elementary students would go home for lunch and then return for the afternoon session. It seems almost impossible that a child could get dismissed at noon, walk home, be fed, and return for the afternoon session by 1:00 pm. We, nevertheless, did it, never missing a beat.

As the economy forced one-income families to become

two-income families, that option slowly disappeared, so elementary schools began offering lunches for the students, thus servicing them in the building for the entire school day. This change occurred in the early 1960s. I remember this because before this happened, my grandfather would pick me up for lunch and take me to my aunt's home, where we would have lunch, after which he would drive me back to school. All this in one hour.

The only students who took buses were those who lived beyond the set distance, which was usually around a mile. Those distances have shrunk over the years due to parental pressure and a basic fear for the safety of the young students who are forced to walk. It has almost taken a complete 180-degree turn to the point where not only do most students get a bus ride to school (unless their backyard abuts the school parking lot), but they are now also picked up at the end of their driveway instead of a central pick-up spot for all neighborhood students. This has resulted in a generation of out-of-shape youths who walk nowhere and are in fear of every person who is not a close friend or relative.

Remember, if you will, that children have been somewhat coddled in their elementary school years. They were told when they could go to the bathroom and, in some cases, escorted by the teacher in a line to the little boys' or little girls' rooms. This would usually happen in the lower grades. Once the child was able to figure out where the boys' and girls' bathrooms were, they could make that walk on their own, usually carrying some bulky object as their bathroom pass. This was great until one child lost the bathroom pass, at which point all visits were terminated until a new pass could be fashioned by the teacher.

Then there was the small cubby in the back of the room where the children were able to keep all their worldly possessions. This might include hats, jackets, backpacks, winter boots, etc. Nothing more appealing than that damp, dank smell of wet jackets, gloves, and winter boots infesting small cubbies for the seven-hour school day. Some of the classrooms might have had racks on which the children would hang their coats.

This system was probably as complicated as any elementary student could handle. Keep in mind that they have been told by Mommy or Daddy what to wear daily and, in some cases, had before they left the house, their coats put on them and properly zipped up to make sure that the cold weather did not cause any germs to infiltrate those tiny creatures. They were asked to do almost nothing in their daily routine. Everything was done for them for a period of five years of school.

Once elementary schools began serving lunch, the students would be systematically walked to the cafeteria in complete silence so as not to interrupt any other classes in session. Once they arrived, they would be herded into seats to eat their lunch or to pick up milk or juice. Those students who were brave enough could make their way to the lunch line and could choose (yes, they were able to choose) their lunch. Once the half-hour lunch was over, the teacher or teacher's aide would pick them up and walk them silently back to their class for the afternoon subjects. Everything was done for them, allowing for very little self-thought or individual decision-making. That would come later in middle school with little or no preparation.

Middle School
and Lockers

Let's talk about middle school lockers for a bit. Keep in mind that the average sixth grader entering middle school has probably never had to deal with keeping their life and room organized. With some assistance from Dad, most of that job has fallen on Mom. If you have ever entered the bedroom of a young adolescent, then you know to what I am referring. Their rooms are mostly unkempt, with all their worldly possessions strewn about the floor and bed. There is hardly any room to walk on the floor without stepping on some article of clothing that has been left there by the youngster, who hopes that someone else might pick it up and wash it. That person usually is the Mom, who has the job of doing the washing and transferring the clothes to the dryer.

Elementary school students are mostly satisfied with whatever has been chosen for them by their parents. If they have clothes on their back, they are happy with the process. Most of the children have free ironing service, compliments of Mom or Dad, along with their clothes neatly put away in their drawers. The children have bought absolutely none of their clothes and thus have little respect for their value. Don't get me wrong. They are glad to have the clothes but cannot possibly realize how much money has been spent to keep them clad in the latest fashion.

Now, we take those children, send them to middle school, give them a locker that measures eight inches wide by four feet high with a small shelf at the top, and ask them to keep it organized and neat. Good luck with that!!! If that isn't enough, we give them a combination lock and ask them to figure out how to open it. Have you ever opened one of those combination locks? Turn left to the first number, then turn the lock to the right going past the first number to the second number, and then left again to a third number. Then pull the lock, and it will open. Yeah, sure. You need an MIT degree to figure this out, yet we expect a twelve-year-old to be able to navigate this task. What is that adage? "It's not rocket science." Oh, it's much more difficult than rocket science; trust me. As an adult, I still have difficulty opening one of those locks.

Once the child gets the locker opened, they must somehow figure out how to fit all his or her books, notebooks, laptop, bookbag, gym clothes, lunch, and any other personal items that they feel they need to bring to school daily. Remember, these are the same children who, two months ago, had their clothes laid out on their bed for them because they had no idea what shirt or blouse matched what pants or skirt they were wearing that day.

If this wasn't difficult enough, the students are usually only allowed to stop at their lockers ONCE during the day, usually mid-morning just before lunch. At that time, they must drop off their paraphernalia from the morning classes and pick up whatever they may need for the rest of the day. It's no wonder that so many of them come to their classes without their homework from the previous night. Oh, they did the work. It is somehow buried at the bottom of the locker with the books or notebooks from the morning classes, never to be found until sometime in June when the locker cleanout happens. In order to make life a little less stressful for middle schoolers, many middle schools will do a mid-year locker cleanout. This usually happens just before Christmas break. If not for this mid-year cleanout, the students in middle school would not be able to close their lockers by March.

The next dilemma is food and lockers. These two items do not blend well with each other. Many students will bring their lunch to school. Then, the daily menu goes up in their homeroom, at which time they realize that their favorite food is being served that day in the cafeteria: Pizza and tater tots—so much for the lunch that Mom and Dad packed for them. That can stay in the locker for consumption later. Unfortunately, that later time never comes. Days and weeks go by, and the bag that was near the top of the locker begins to make its way down to the bottom, slowly being buried under a swarm of books, papers, and gym clothes. Most people don't know this, but it is a proven fact that peanut butter, when left alone in a locker for three months, WILL turn to stone! There is written proof in history journals indicating that the Great Pyramids were, indeed, made from peanut butter. Just kidding!!

One little tidbit concerning middle school lockers:

After every school year, on the first day of summer break, the custodian and I would go through all the lockers in the school and empty all the clothes that were left by the students. We needed to do this, so the custodians could properly clean out the lockers in preparation for the next school year. This was my favorite day of the year. I literally would do all my clothes shopping for the upcoming year. I had, at my disposal, clothes from GAP, American Eagle, Tommy Bahamas, and Aeropostale. Those clothes would be taken home, washed, and neatly hung in my closet for wearing the following season. I, of course, never wore any of those clothes to school the following year for fear that a student might possibly recognize their long, lost shirt now being worn by the Assistant Principal.

Covid added another monkey wrench into the middle school experience. When the schools were deemed safe enough for students to return, some schools took out the lockers for fear that they were another breeding ground for possible infection. Now, instead of having students dealing with lockers and the organizational skills that go with them, there are hundred-pound students carrying everything for the entire day in a backpack. If you haven't picked up one of your children's backpacks lately, give it a try. Those suckers are beyond heavy. All their books for the entire day are heavy enough. Add to that weight your coat in winter and any other things that previously were stored in your locker. Three years of carrying that backpack around is certainly a recipe for spinal stenosis. I'm all for a rigorous activity for our young, but this borders on child cruelty.

I was recently talking with my grandson, who is finishing middle school and will be going to high school next year. He has never had a locker in middle school. Instead, he holds everything for school in his backpack. On occasion, I picked him up and made the mistake of grabbing his backpack for him when arriving at his home. I cannot understand how a young adolescent can carry that much weight around their back all day without developing some physical side effects. He is a strong young boy, who is not slight in stature. Many of the young females who weigh eighty-five pounds at most carry the same number of books in their backpacks. That is the equivalent of a person carrying almost seventy-five percent of their weight around all day. This can't possibly be good for anyone going through a major growth spurt, as most middle schoolers are.

Middle School and Physical Education

Physical Education in American middle schools has gotten away from us, to say the least. I don't want to sound like an old person complaining that the youngsters of today don't have to do anything to demonstrate any physical prowess. Because of restraints that have been put in place concerning the liability of schools and teachers, most real physical education is no longer possible. Gone are the days of students learning how to master any kind of athletic skill with the fear of failing to reach any kind of goal. Teachers can't teach wrestling for fear of an injury to the student and pending legal action, can't play dodgeball because a student might claim that he or she are being targeted because of their gender choices, can't climb the ropes for fear of a fall and more legal action. Are you getting my point? All that is left in PE class is wiffle ball or softball in the spring, walking the track in the nice weather, or soccer for those who wish to participate. It doesn't take long for a student to figure out that if they conveniently forget their PE uniform, they will not be able to participate. In the colder months, basketball is a staple for PE class. That is usually dominated by two or three players who are part of an AAU travel team. Nobody else ever sees the ball.

In elementary school, the children were taken outside—when the weather permitted—and played fun games like kickball or maybe jump rope. There may be a little jogging to get the blood flowing, but any strenuous exercise is strongly frowned upon. Physical education, thus, at the elementary school level, is more of a forty-five-minute respite for the classroom teachers to gather themselves while a physical education teacher helps the students rid themselves of any pent-up energy that may have built up during the day.

Now, we take those same children and send them off to middle school. Their first physical education class becomes an introduction to real organized sports. Sure, they have played some town sports with Mom or Dad as their coach. Now, PE in middle school becomes a bit of a reality check for some of the first-year middle schoolers. In town recreation leagues, they may have found themselves to be budding stars at that age level. Suddenly, in some communities, all the sixth graders in the town are attending the same school setting up a totally new level of competition. The students are instructed to have a physical education "uniform"—consisting of matching-colored shirts and shorts—usually the color of the school mascot. Those PE uniforms can usually be purchased at some local sports store for a conveniently overpriced amount. The great thing about PE uniforms is that you never have to remember to pack any extra clothes for PE. The bad part is that most new middle school students don't bother to bring their new PE uniform home for proper laundering. It becomes so much more convenient to merely stuff it in their new locker for use the next time they have physical education class. Fast forward a month into the school year and to that PE class. Pity the poor teacher who must deal with thirty students who have figured out the "PE clothes in the locker" scheme. That smell, even in a large gymnasium, can be nauseating.

Those new sixth graders will also be introduced to the concept of middle school Interscholastic Team sports. Although rare, most of the sixth graders usually have a difficult time making the school team. That honor is usually saved for the seventh and eighth graders who have paid their dues sitting on the bench their first year. For some of these children, this becomes their first real confrontation with rejection. Until now, Mom and Dad had given them false hope that they would someday be the next LeBron James or Pele. Their town athletic experience had been a skewed example of how school sports really work. No longer does everyone get a ribbon or trophy for simply participating. Winning now becomes paramount for a school coach who is collecting a paycheck for his toils. This experience then becomes Dad's first encounter with "the coach"!! In some smaller communities, Dad may already know the coach from town sports. If this isn't the case, it can become a rather uncomfortable meeting. Dad has been telling the child how great he or she is, so now he must back up all this praise by going to the school and lobbying on behalf of his child. This usually doesn't turn out well for the Dad or the child. As a former high school soccer coach for over twenty years, I have seen this scenario repeatedly. The best one of these came near the end of my coaching career. My assistant coach and I had heard about this promising player coming into the school for his first year. After we had run our first couple of practice sessions, we had a male parent come up to us at the end of practice, take us both aside, and tell us, "You want my son on the field." We very politely acknowledged him and said we would take a good hard look at his son. After he left, I remember just looking at my assistant and shaking my head. We could not believe the boldness of this parent, who took the concept of lobbying for a child to new heights. The crazy thing about this kid was that once we started putting the players in game situations, he was the one player we, indeed, did want on the field. He wound up starting for us for four years.

In middle school, the normal progression is to maybe make the team as a sixth grader, sit on the bench to observe and learn, and then play as a seventh and eighth grader. Still, it is a reality check for many of these young kids. Some of them become so devastated by the failure to make the team that they stop playing the sport altogether.

Most middle schools will add a health component to their PE curriculum, hoping to educate the young students on the ills of drugs, the overuse of steroids, youth pregnancy and social diseases, proper nutrition, and the like. For many of these sixth graders, this may be their first introduction to such material. They may have led a somewhat sheltered life, where the parents chose not to tell them about these things for fear of exposing them to negative ideas and thoughts. One can only imagine the questions at the supper table after one of those lessons.

13

When I was an Assistant Principal at the middle school level, I had, on numerous occasions, the pleasure of students who had been sent to my office for refusing to take PE. The reasons were often lame and too silly to even mention. I had one young lady who spent an entire quarter of physical education class sitting in my class doing her homework. She, of course, did not pass the class. Some schools have made it mandatory for students to pass Physical Education classes to ensure they attend.

Middle School Dress Codes and Physical Changes

This chapter will be a bit of a split between middle school dress codes and the growth spurts that occur with adolescents during these formative years. I will first deal with the growth spurts of young boys and girls in middle school and how it impacts their social experience. To better explain this, picture, if you would, sixth graders and how they look when entering middle school. They are still in their formative years and have yet to develop fully physically. Let's talk about females first.

Most females will experience their fastest growth spurt during the ages of eleven or twelve. Depending on when the female starts menstruation, she will probably grow another two or three inches. Also factored in will be diet and nutrition. For the most part, most females will reach their adult height around age fourteen or fifteen. With females also comes the blossoming of breasts. This will vary with girls depending on when they start menstruation. This physical change usually causes self-conscious feelings of now having breasts. It is not hard to see that many of these young female adolescents are quite uncomfortable with their new body image. Others will embrace this new, more mature look by flaunting it every chance they get. Gone are the old training bras, now replaced by fancy bras that are sometimes too sophisticated for someone their age.

Suddenly, all the fashion decisions that were once left to Mom and Dad become paramount in the daily life of these young female adolescents. Gone are all the kiddie magazines, now replaced by Teen, Vogue, and any other periodical that will influence the dress and style of these young girls. The only problem with all of this is that these same young girls are nowhere near ready to assume the bodies of young ladies. Their brains are still those of little girls who need to be guided and taught almost everything that will occur in these adolescent years. Looking the part of a growing, young woman can lead to disaster when they have no idea how to handle the attention that this new physical presence will bring. All would be fine if they could dress up and stand still in front of a mirror. Unfortunately, they must now learn to walk properly in heels, sit properly in a dress, and regulate the amount of makeup they put on their face. This task is not something that happens overnight. It takes them months and, in some cases, years to figure out how to navigate these tasks. In the meantime, they struggle mightily, attempting to fit in with all the other females in their class. Body image becomes the one and only thing they care about. Everywhere they look, they view models characterizing how they need to look. These young girls fail to differentiate between fantasy and reality. Their attempt to portray themselves as those they view as role models fails to symbolize their youth.

These unattainable goals are magnified by social media sites that they visit on a regular basis. For every twenty sites displaying slim, tanned, professionally made-up young girls, there may be only one or two sites that offer encouragement for these girls to feel comfortable in their own bodies. The role models they look up to, like Taylor Swift, Beyonce, and Rihanna, are so different from the females with whom they associate with. Yet, they believe the false narrative that they, too, can look and dress like these superstars. It will be much later in life before they realize that true beauty comes from within and that outward appearances mean little in the real world.

Another issue that comes with middle school students and their dress style is the fact that their parents will more than likely totally disagree with the choices these youngsters make regarding what they wear to school. This is where the newly discovered backpack plays an important camouflage for the young teen. The scenario goes like this: First, the young female middle schooler puts on what they want to wear to school. Next, they make their way down to breakfast, only to have a parent send them back to their room to change into something more appropriate. Now, they use their newfound intelligence to secretly place their desired outfit in their backpack, change back into the clothes that Mom or Dad approve of, and make their way to school, only to change in the ladies' room back

17

into the outfit that they wanted to wear in the first place. This usually works until that one time when their outfit is so inappropriate that their parents are called by the school asking them to bring in a change of clothes for their daughter. Remember, these young teens think that they have all the answers and have covered all the bases, only to realize that their parents attempted to pull all the same cons when they were young.

It is very difficult for anyone with a position of authority in middle school to guide these young ladies in the area of proper dress. In a perfect world, we would be able to have school uniforms for all students. This would eliminate the need for students to dress up to the standards of others in their class. Private and parochial schools have uniforms, and it takes away any competition between those students whose parents have the means to buy nicer, more appropriate clothes and those from less fortunate households. This is quite impossible since first amendment rights activists claim that students should have the right to express themselves by dressing how they choose. When a female student is sent down to the office for wearing inappropriate clothing, it is a very difficult position for the administrator. As an Assistant Principal, female students were regularly sent to me because they had skirts that were too short, tops that were too revealing, or pants with rips in inappropriate areas. There was very little that I could say to the girls since whatever observation I made could be viewed as sexual harassment. Luckily, I had a female school nurse, a female social worker, and two female school psychologists working for me. They were immediately called in, and I would defer to them for any female discussions on dress codes. I sometimes referred to them as "wife number two and wife number three" since they saved me from many uncomfortable situations with young female adolescents.

Boys are much easier to handle when it comes to dress code violations and growth spurt issues. Because males grow at a steadier pace and don't finish growing until almost eighteen to twenty-one, the only issue they may have in middle school is a drastic change in their voice. That young male voice will be steadily replaced with a more manly voice. If they are lucky, most of this change will happen during the summer. This way, they will not have to deal with those sudden unexpected squeaky sounds that make their way out of their mouths.

During the three years of middle school, males usually start to develop hair on their faces, under their arms and legs, and around their genitals. Little attention is paid to the development of these young boys. They are much less concerned with physical appearance and could care less what they are wearing. This is never more apparent than during special school events when they are forced to dress up. When I say dress up, I mean that their jeans will not have holes in the legs or backside area. If it is suggested to them that they wear a collared shirt and tie, they become totally bemused. I cannot tell you how many young men have come to me to help them fix their ties before a semi-formal event. They have no idea how to tie a tie and, in most cases, don't even own a tie. I would usually have a stash of old ties I no longer wore and would give them to the young men to use. For the most part, males in middle school are content wearing jeans, tees, sweatpants, sweatshirts, and sneakers. The brand of sneakers is probably the only item of clothing they may care about. Everything else is just fluff. The most annoying problem for teachers and administrators at the middle school level with boys is the saggy pants issue. They still insist on wearing their jeans far below their waist. How they manage to keep them from falling off is a problem for the physics teacher. Most of them can barely walk with their pants below their waist. Running with pants at this level is almost impossible.

Growing at such a rapid rate during middle school usually comes with some drawbacks. The boys are usually very clumsy, and it is not at all unusual to have them trip over their own feet as they walk down the corridor. This usually goes away once most of their growing ends, but that is something that will not occur until sometime in high school. It's quite amazing to see the changes in a young male adolescent four years later. Some of them may grow almost a foot in those four years. They are almost unnoticeable if they come back to the school to pick up a younger sibling.

As I mentioned in another chapter, at the end of the school year, I would help the custodian empty out the lockers. Most of the clothing that I confiscated was that of male students. The females always had to make sure that those outfits that were in their lockers made their way home so Mom and Dad didn't find out that they were changing upon their arrival at school.

Cell Phones
in Middle School

As if middle school wasn't difficult enough, we have now added another form of distraction to complicate the adolescent mind: the Cell Phone. Don't get me wrong. I am appreciative of the fact that any information that I need can be instantly retrieved because of the great strides in technology. However, does an eleven- or twelve-year-old really need to carry a cell phone during the school day? I know they have probably given their parents numerous reasons why their phone is a necessity for their safety both during and after school. The problem arises when that same youngster is using their phone to visit sites like Twitter, Tik Tok, Instagram, and many others available to them at any time of the day. Remember how I said that the brain of a middle school student is still in the developmental stages? Are we to believe that they have the common sense to distinguish what is real and what is fake on these sites? Do they know the negative implications of what they may post on these various sites and how these posts never ever go away? I think not.

Most bullying that occurs in middle schools is not the result of face-to-face confrontations. Most of these problems are a direct result of things that have been posted after school or during the weekend. The one constant characteristic of middle school students is that they don't possess the reasoning ability to understand that things that are said or done in the present have long-term consequences. Why is this so? It is this way because middle school students live in the here and now. Everything is today. For them, there is no tomorrow, no future, no long-term plan. Ask most middle school students where they see themselves in five or ten years, and you will get a blank stare as if you have asked them to solve a quantum physics problem. When faced with emotional or personal problems, they fall apart, unable to take a breath and realize that this will pass, and things will be better. Now we put a cell phone in their possession and expect them to use it in a responsible manner. That is not going to happen.

Most of the students in this age group have a very difficult time expressing their feelings verbally. It has become so much easier to say what needs to be said on a cell phone and in the privacy of one's bedroom where there are no others present to look you in the eye and refute what you just said. This problem was compounded during Covid when cell phones were the one way to stay in contact with their friends. There was no fear of getting infected with the virus through cell phone contact. Loneliness and home confinement only added fuel to the fire. The cell phone and the middle schooler were a bad mix that only got worse during Covid. There was too much time to view sites not meant for the adolescent mind to comprehend.

The idea of taking phones away from this population is an idea that will not work. "The horse is already out of the barn," as they say. What needs to be done is this. Schools need to restrict the use of cell phones during classroom hours. There is no need for any middle school student to use their phone while in class. Some braver, forward-thinking school systems have put policies in place that ban the use of cell phones during school hours. Phones are off and out of sight during classroom time. Some systems have allowed students to be on their phones during lunch, but this only creates more problems for the administrators in charge, who must ensure phones are off when the students leave the cafeteria. Who forgets to turn it off? Who makes that one more call or post before the next class begins? Just turn off the phone for the entire school day, so many problems are solved.

I saw where one middle school recently had a school dance, and no phones were allowed at the dance. This decision finally gave the middle schoolers time to talk and interact with each other on a new and more personal level—with their voices. The students had what appeared to be a great time. All pressure was off them to post or take offensive pictures of others. This needs to be done more with this age group. If we don't do this, we risk creating a group of adults who cannot communicate with others in a civil and calm manner.

Middle School Lunch

Many changes have occurred in education during the last fifty years, but none more dramatic to an adolescent than the jump from elementary school to middle school. When junior high school was changed from grades seven through nine to grades six through eight and renamed middle school, the way a child was taught had to change accordingly. We were teaching students who were a year younger when they entered the school and a year younger when they left. With that age difference came a maturity level that was also lacking. We need to remember that the human brain of an adolescent is still developing at that age and has not even come close to where it will be as an adult. Add to that equation the physical and emotional changes of the child, and you have a recipe for disaster. The major difference between elementary and middle school is basically the amount of independence and responsibility thrust upon these eleven and thirteen-year-olds.

Let's take a short look at lunch. This phenomenon still boggles my mind. We, as educators, expect a young person to, in twenty-two minutes, get to the cafeteria, line up, get lunch, eat it, and return to class, impacting the digestive system in what must be a negative way. Too bad if you must make a bathroom visit during that time. Should you have a class at the far end of the building, you would have little or no chance of completing both lunch and bathroom visits without throwing half of your lunch in the garbage.

In order to keep some sort of order in the cafeteria, I would often have students all come in and sit at the table of their choice. Once that task was accomplished, students would be called up to the food line by the table. This was meant to keep the line shorter and allowed me to hold back a table where the students were being noisy or not behaving. This method worked for control, but it also had a negative impact on the students who sat at the table that was called last. They might only have ten minutes to eat their lunch. There is a yin and yang for every decision you make when you are an Assistant Principal in charge of lunch duty.

I remember when I was in junior high school, there was a student who would get his lunch, bring it to his seat in the cafeteria, and then leave to go to the bathroom before he ate. I'm not sure if he went to wash his hands before eating or doing his business. Every day was the same routine. I can't even imagine leaving an unsupervised lunch tray on a table in the cafeteria today for one minute, never mind five minutes, and then having the confidence to return and eat the food on that tray. Today, that food would surely be tampered with by some prankster in middle school who was looking to impress their friends at the table. Keep in mind that when I was in junior high school, kids were a little more fearful of doing something that might have gotten them sent to the office. Back then, that fact might have saved the lunch of the student.

Today, most middle school students will either have a bagged lunch or an account with the local lunch provider. At the beginning of the school year, your guardian puts money into an account. The student is then given an ID which they show at the end of the food line, where the appropriate amount is deducted from the account. Students are given an update on their accounts at various times during the year. At that time, they can have their parents or guardians put more money back into the account. Then we have students with free and reduced school lunches. They qualify for free or reduced lunch based on family income. This creates added pressure on those students since they are now viewed as poor. At the middle school level, this becomes just another thing over whichstudents can be verbally bullied.

Because most middle schoolers live in their own little world, they have neither the maturity nor common sense to keep track of their lunch account balance. Their main concern is the lunch on their tray. They have little concern over when the next payment is due. Some students have figured out how to "double bag it." They take lunch from home and then buy a hot lunch from the cafeteria. After all, they are growing young adolescents. This would not be a problem in a perfect world. Covid changed all that. With so many people losing their jobs during Covid, governments offered free lunches to all students for a specified time. Students now became used to going up and getting what they wanted without any thought of having to pay for it. Not too long ago, the free money for lunches ended.

Unfortunately, the appetites of the middle school student didn't end. These mindless individuals failed to realize that the free food they had been taking advantage of for two years was now ending. It might have been a good idea to let Mom and Dad know they needed to replenish their food account at the school. That would be way too responsible an act to expect from a middle school student. Suddenly, you have parents getting bills from the lunch provider, requesting payment of back bills for all those lunches that their little cherub charged to the account.

The end of lunch in middle school can be a stressful time for the adults who oversee keeping order for 150 or so students. The tables are usually clean and neat when the students arrive for lunch. There is very little garbage of any sort on the floor. The tables, floor, and trash barrels have been quickly cleaned and emptied by the custodial staff. This all happens in less than five minutes. By the end of lunch, the cafeteria appears as if some type of food typhoon has struck it. There is garbage everywhere. It's as if the students were under the impression that Mom was there to clean up. I would always dismiss by the table. No table was allowed to leave until the table and floor under it were clean and free of litter. My favorite saying was, "Your mother doesn't live here. Clean up after yourselves."

Most of this cafeteria craziness diminishes in high school. There are usually food stations where the more mature customer can choose from a variety of different choices. Also, many of the high school students are paying for the food with money from their small, part-time jobs. Unfortunately, this book is about middle school, so the lunchroom mania continues for the time being.

Who Gets the Parents

Middle school is usually the time in a child's life when the thought of going out on a date becomes a possibility. Some middle schoolers are physically and emotionally more advanced, so that first date may come sooner rather than later. This small chapter is not so much about middle school dating but more so about how it directly affects the parents of the two dating children.

From the time the child starts school in first grade, friends begin to play a larger part in their lives. Little by little, through elementary school, the child will meet and become friendly with numerous other classmates. Then, by the coaxing of the child, play dates are arranged by both parents. If the child participates in one of the numerous sponsored athletic leagues the town runs, he or she will make more new friends. Then their circle of friends becomes larger and larger, at which time, the parents feel obligated to introduce themselves to the parents of these new friends whom their child has made. These parental friendships usually last for the elementary school years. All those friendships change when the child goes to middle school.

When a child gets to middle school, he or she will be put on an academic team. Those teams will likely stay together for the three years the child attends school. The only time this will change is when a parent of a student requests a change of team for their child due to personality conflicts with the team of teachers or if a student has been misplaced at the beginning of the term. At that point, the student might begin to make new friends who will become their new "crew." Some of the old friends, with whom they were very close, might slowly drift away, and they understandably may make new friends.

This would be a normal transformation if it were not for the fact that we are dealing with middle schoolers. Their emotions are like a roller coaster ride: up one day, down the next. When, thereafter, Mom and Dad ask their daughter why she doesn't hang around with her old friend Suzy any longer, they are told that Suzy isn't quite cool enough for their daughter, so she has decided to find new, more interesting friends. None of this is at all unusual. It happens all the time in a child's school years. They change friends often for many reasons. The female species is more social than the male. They wear their hearts on their sleeves. Boys will tuck their emotions away in a pocket somewhere and seldom will be overly concerned by these changes in friends.

I remember when my wife and I took one of my daughter's or son's friends with us on some family vacations. These vacations were not your two-day, one-night excursions to the next state. We're talking about a full week at Disney, complete with the park passes, food costs, and other entertainment fees. We even took one of our daughter's friends on a week-long cruise. These trips both occurred when the children were in elementary school and had not yet expanded their base of friends. That would come a short time later when they started middle school. Once that transition to middle school happened, the girls found new friends and, little by little, stopped hanging out with each other.

This is not a traumatic issue for the children. They are far more resilient than we, the adults, are. The bigger issue is with the parents. When the children move on to other friends or break up after dating someone for a while, who gets the parents? What I mean is that the parents, over time, have built a nice bond with each other. They may go out to dinner together, play cards, or even take a dual family summer vacation together. Now that little Suzy and Jane have moved on to new friends in middle school, WHO GETS THE PARENTS? It becomes rather awkward for the parents to continue socializing with one another when their children stop being friends. This can be a worse breakup than the actual adolescent breakup. After all, the two couples enjoyed each other's company for quite some time as well as built a great relationship. Now, their conversations are limited when it comes to their children. This result is a strained conversation at the restaurant when your two children no longer hang around with each other.

I assume that parents, who home-school their middle school children, don't have this issue. They probably don't have many friends outside their family circle and may be very protective with whom their children associate. Isn't that the reason that they home-schooled their kids in the first place?

When everything is said and done, we, the parents, meet and lose adult friends because our middle school children are very fickle with whom they associate with and date as they go through those adolescent years as young teens.

Middle School
and Covid

Covid had a profound effect on the public schools in our country and many other countries around the world. It is estimated that schoolchildren lost approximately two to three years of education during the pandemic. The government decided on remote learning to keep the students and teachers safe from being contaminated. This was all well and good, but we must realize the results that this decision produced. The one area that attracted most of our attention was the loss of knowledge that failed to reach the students. This loss of education was felt from elementary school through high school. Programs were dummied down in order to "teach" the students over the Internet. Some courses were terminated because they could not realistically be taught through Zoom classes. There was little ability to have a constant give and take necessary for more technical courses like trigonometry, physics, and advanced math and science classes.

Dominating the loss of all learning material was the

more crucial loss of interpersonal skills. Take a society built on communication, then remove the ability to perform face-to-face communication, and you are left with a personality void that spans an entire generation. We were forced to take young adolescents and keep them away from the stimulus they most desired: their friends and classmates. This sudden and prolonged stretch of isolation from their peers must have had a negative effect on an entire population of young students. The one age group which suffered the most had to be the middle schoolers. Why is this so? Look at a picture from the yearbook of a fifth grader at any elementary school. Then, look at a picture of that same student in the eighth grade. I would guess that, in many cases, the two students would not look alike. The physical and emotional changes that occur during the middle school years are astonishing. Not only do middle school students make massive leaps in physical appearance, but their emotional state of mind is also in constant flux. If you don't think this is true, then take a ride on a middle school bus full of eleven–thirteen-year-olds. Come into the cafeteria in the morning and listen to 400 middle school students await the start of the school day. Much is spoken, but little is of any social value. Remember, now you are dealing with a group of young people who are social beings. They are between the elementary years, when they will still talk to their parents, and the high school years, when they will answer their parents will terse, one-word answers like "fine," "good," or my favorite, "whatever." Middle schoolers will constantly talk your ear off. The only problem is that very little of what they say makes any sense.

Now Covid enters the scene, and these social beings

are taken away from all human interaction with their peers for an extended period. This does not include the Internet. (Don't even get me started on that aspect of their lives). Covid ends, and we have a segment of our population (middle schoolers) who not only have lost two years of learning their academics but also many of the social interaction skills necessary to survive in this world. Remember that a middle school student's brain and thought processes are still developing and will not be fully matured for at least another five or six years. Now, the unfiltered material that comes out of middle school students' mouths before is now even more unfiltered because they have been talking to nobody but themselves for two years, and to themselves, they make total sense. It's just the rest of us who walk around shaking our heads when they speak.

Many of these students must work very hard trying to determine how to interact with the rest of the world properly. You see, the entire universe centers around them and them alone. Nothing outside of the imaginary three-foot bubble that surrounds them is of any importance. Their world is one of "me," "I," "mine," and any other personal pronoun you know. Thus, the greatest challenge for middle schoolers today is to somehow figure out the proper way to interact with the rest of humanity. Covid took that away from many of them.

Another group of middle school students who were severely affected was the special education students of this age. Before Covid, they fought for all the services they sorely needed. Then, they lost most of those services from the school and were dependent on Mom and Dad to fill in the gaps. Most parents are not qualified to do that job, which puts more stress on the middle school student receiving special education services. They, unfortunately, fell even further behind the curve. It will be necessary for the leaders of our educational system to work very hard to restore what was lost during those two years of Covid.

Middle School
& Gender Choices

This will be a shorter chapter because I'm not quite
sure how to deal with it. Remember how I said that the
students coming from a somewhat sheltered existence
in elementary school are suddenly thrust into this new
world of change upon entering middle school? In addition
to this new world of change with expectations of more
autonomy/independence, society has now evolved to
more publicly recognize the fluidity of gender identity and
sexual preferences that have existed since the beginning
of time. We now have a population of students (male and
female) who are struggling or experimenting, trying to
figure out where they fit on the gender identity spectrum.
Some students already feel different from their peers yet
want to fit in. Not only is entering middle school a huge
challenge, but the physical and emotional changes are
continuing. Figuring out one's gender identity or sexual
preference is scary, and the fear of being ostracized,
bullied, discriminated against, abandoned, or rejected

by parents and teachers is real for them. It is a confusing time for all parties.

Let's take a quick look at what we, as adults, expect these young adolescents to remember and understand. We all know about the acronym LGBTQIA+. This stands for Lesbian, Gay, Bisexual, Transexual, Queer, Intersex, and Asexual. I find it interestingly crazy that the powers to be found it necessary to add a "+" sign to this list. Is this just in case we have not been able to identify every gender group on the planet? We have groups of he/him/his and she/her/hers. Truly, the acronym LGBTQIA and reassigning or adopting pronoun usage that may more aptly describe who they are, is different from what we were taught and confusing to us. For some, at the ripe age of eleven or twelve, the adolescent's own choice of gender preferences or sexual orientation can be in flux or experimentation and may be very different at a later time in their lives. Some students don't make those decisions until later in life. Misgendering has taken up so much of the school curriculum and class time that there isn't enough time left to conquer the core subjects. Having just left elementary school, most middle school students are struggling just to survive the new daily life experiences. Let's make it even more stressful for them by forcing them to make gender choices that they are in no way ready to make.

As of 2021, misgendering, which is purposefully or mistakenly calling another student by the wrong pronoun, is punishable by school suspension. This was first employed in Virginia schools but has now made its way across the country. I am in no way attempting to be political when it comes to this subject. I do think that we need to spend more time educating our children on subject matters that will serve them going forward. Again, I repeat myself by stating that middle school students do not have the cognitive ability to make these life-altering decisions at their age. They might change their minds about their sexual orientation twice or thrice in the three years they spend in middle school.

One of the newest dilemmas confronting the administration of these schools is what bathroom each student should use. Gone are the days when you went to the boy's or girl's bathroom. Middle school students must now choose between boys', girls', or gender-neutral bathrooms. Hell, it takes them the entire first quarter of the year just to find out where the bathrooms are! What are we doing to these kids? If bathroom choices are such a big deal in order to be "politically correct," then have three-bathroom designations: those for boys, those for girls, and those for gender-neutral bathrooms. Allow the students to choose what bathroom they feel most comfortable using. Let's spend less time on bathrooms and more time on the major subjects that we lost during the two years of Covid home learning.

I am not targeting this population in any way. I believe all children are God's children and must be treated equally. Let's not make it more stressful for students dealing with gender identity and sexual preferences. Ultimately, we ought to try offering them support, unbiased therapy if wanted or needed, and a safer environment in which to be who they are, not only with gender identity but also as people contributing to the good of society. We need to find new ways to let them know that they are accepted unconditionally, no matter what their gender choices are. Let's not overload these middle schoolers with too much pressure to make life-changing decisions at this early age. Proper counseling needs to be offered to help assist students in the choices they make. It cannot be viewed as a problem but needs to be viewed as another step in the development of our younger generation. An interesting quote comes from Alice Hoffman, author of *The Rules of Magic*: "What if I don't want to be what I am?" "Then you will face a life of unhappiness." We have enough unhappiness in our world. Let's not add any more.

Conclusion

What I have tried to do in this short book is to high-light some of the challenges of middle school for young adolescents who must endure these for three years. Some of the topics are more humorous than others, and some of them are of a more serious nature. If this were some sort of science fiction, futuristic novel, the children of middle school age would probably be sent to some remote island to farm rice for three years. The gist of the story is that most of the youngsters who enter middle school are in no way prepared for the events that they will face daily, including intense emotional and physical changes. This is not to say that the elementary schools are not preparing them properly. They do. But they have little control over human physiology.

Because this is the real world, we should take a closer look into the characters about whom we are writing. Who, then, are these children? They are your children, and they are mine. They look just like us, act just like us, and will, in most cases, grow up to be carbon copies of their parents. For the three years of middle school, they are children with whom we are constantly at odds. Why is that? Suddenly, these children, who are mostly mirror images of us, become like aliens from another planet. They are cruel to each other. They will cry at the drop of a hat since every situation in their lives is catastrophic in nature. On the other hand, they will donate their time to any charity if it means being in the company of their peers. The reason for the fundraiser is secondary to them. Most importantly is that they are with the other members of their social group, which is paramount to their existence. Their lives are like rollercoasters: up as high as the sky one day and plunging down to earth the next. Sometimes, their personality changes daily. Other times they can be moment to moment. The adults in their lives are merely custodians left to pick up the pieces from the wreckage they have caused.

What do they need to survive this turmoil of middle school? They need love and comfort from any of the adults in their life. That may seem easy to provide. After all, we truly love all our children "to the moon and back." There is nothing that we would not do for them, no pain that we would not take from them, and no burden of theirs that we would not put upon ourselves to make their lives easier. Notice how I said, LOVE. We LOVE these children, but during those middle school years, they make it very difficult to LIKE them. It becomes an extremely difficult task dealing with the mood swings, verbal outbursts, and basic breakdown in what was once a great parent-child relationship for the first ten years of the adolescent's life.

What we all need to do is to take a step back and realize that these adolescents will, at some point, come around to a normal way of thinking and behaving. Patience is what is needed—miles and miles of patience on the part of the adults during this journey. This can often be a very difficult endeavor for parents and teachers. It's easy to tell people to be patient with these adolescents unless you are in the trenches with them and must deal with them daily.

Because we are looking at middle schoolers, it is important to remember that they will be on a team of students with mostly the same teachers for three years. Once you get a reputation within the team, it becomes difficult for the student to lose that reputation, be it good or bad. By year number three, you could be looking at a situation where the teachers on the team are cringing over the thought of another year with Johnny or Susy.

It becomes a scheduling puzzle for the team. Do we put the problem student in a higher-level classroom where they will not have friends to entertain, and the better students will ignore them? Without an audience, the disruptive student will often realize that the other students are not acknowledging their behaviors, and thus, they stop acting out. It is our job to steer them in the right direction in order to ensure that they turn out to be caring adults who will pass on positive values to the world and their children.

Remember what I said about having patience with these adolescents? Patience, as well as love and compassion, will always work. Think back, if you would, to your days in middle school. We all went through the same changes, the same insecurities, and the same growing pains. Yet, if you are reading this, then you somehow made it through all of it. Let's give the youngsters of today the same chance that we all had. If someone along the way had not shown me that same patience and love, I might never have been able to become a somewhat successful adult and probably would not have written this book. One final word of advice: check your middle schooler's cell phones. You will be amazed at what you will find on those little electronic devices!!

About the Author

John LaFauci earned his bachelor's degree from Rhode Island College in Sociology and his master's degree in Secondary School Administration from Providence College. As such, he worked as a History teacher in the Warwick School System for 20 years and a Middle School Administrator in North Providence for 6 years. He was a high school soccer coach at Pilgrim High School and Burrillville High School. In 2008, he was honored in Rhode Island and Washington D.C. as Rhode Island Vice Principal of the Year. He also served on the Smithfield School Committee for four years. He has been married to his wife Joan LaFauci, a former English teacher in Cranston for 28 years. They have been married for 52 years. They have two grown children, Brian LaFauci, a self-employed businessman, who owns a personal consulting company and a real estate holding company. His daughter, Ashlee Barton is a school psychologist in the Smithfield School Department and owns her own spin and fitness studio.

This is his second novel, having written numerous short articles for local magazines. When not writing, John enjoys golf, tennis, and pickleball. Joan and John have done extensive traveling, always looking to broaden their horizons and discover new and interesting places and things. In his free time, he is kept busy attending the athletic events of his two grandchildren, Ava and Cade LaFauci.